Li...
to...

- St. Jude Thaddeus,
  pray for us.

- Bl. Kateri Tekakwitha,
  pray for us.

- St. Maria Goretti,
  pray for us.

- St. Peter Claver,
  pray for us.

- St. Patrick of Ireland,
  pray for us.

- St. Rita of Cascia,
  pray for us.

- St. Tarcisius the Acolyte,
  pray for us.

- My Patron Saint,
  pray for us.

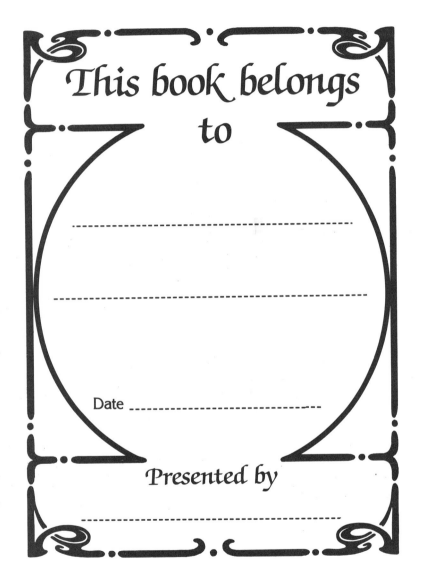

This book belongs
to

Date --

Presented by

PRAYERS
to the
SAINTS

By
FATHER LOVASIK
S.V.D.

NIHIL OBSTAT: James T. O'Connor, S.T.D., Censor Librorum
IMPRIMATUR: ✠ Patrick J. Sheridan, D.D., Vicar General, Archdiocese of New York

The Nihil Obstat and Imprimatur are official declarations that a book or pamphlet is free of doctrinal or moral error. No implication is contained therein that those who have granted the Nihil Obstat and Imprimatur agree with the contents, opinions or statements expressed.

PRAYER TO MARY

Queen of All Saints

D EAR Mary,
loving Mother of God,
Queen of all Saints
and Help of Christians,
assist us.

You are the most blessed of all creatures
and the most beloved by Jesus.

You are our Mother also,
and we are devoted to you.

Mother, as Jesus loved you,
help us to love you.

We are most grateful
that Jesus gave you to us
to be our Mother, our Helper, our Protector.

Please take care of us
and our families and loved ones
and all who are in need.

PRAYER TO ST. JOSEPH

Foster Father of Jesus

O Great St. Joseph,
   you were the husband of the Virgin Mary
   and foster father of Jesus.

During your life on earth,
   you were always obedient
   to the guidance of the Holy Spirit.

Watch over me every day
   just as you watched over Jesus
   when He was growing up.

Obtain for me the grace to know
   what God wants me to be in life,
   because my happiness on earth depends
      on it.

Help me to carry out God's will faithfully
   and to choose the vocation
   that will lead me to heaven.

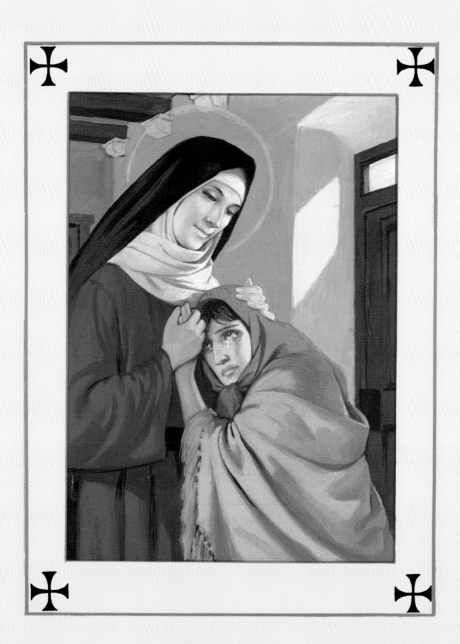

PRAYER TO ST. ANGELA MERICI

Dedicated Teacher

D EAR St. Angela,
  you followed God's inspiration
  to found a new Congregation of Nuns.

You instructed your Nuns
  to teach children about Christ
  and to care for them in His Name.

In our time,
  we are surrounded by all kinds of teachers
  who offer instruction in living.

Help us to follow your example
  and listen only to those
  who teach us to love and follow Christ.

Ask God to send us good teachers
  who will teach His word
  to their students.

Make me a good student
  so that I may learn about God
  and about our world.

PRAYER TO ST. ANTHONY OF PADUA

Patron of the Poor

D EAR St. Anthony,
   you are the patron of the poor
   and the helper of all who seek lost articles.

You also taught us
   the great importance of prayer,
   which puts us in touch with God
   and brings us His help.

Keep me close to God each day
   through my daily prayers.

Help me to be good to my family
   and all my friends.

Come to the aid of all people
   who seek what they have lost—
   especially those who seek
   to regain the grace of God.

PRAYER TO ST. BERNADETTE

Associate of Our Lady of Lourdes

D EAR St. Bernadette,
   when you were only fourteen years old
   you had the privilege of seeing Our Lady
      eighteen times.

Because of your faith,
   the shrine of Lourdes was built
   and became world-famous for its cures.

You became a Nun and suffered much
   for the glory of God.

Teach me to be patient and understanding
   toward all people.

Give me a great love for Mary
   and her Divine Son Jesus.

Let me pray to her daily
   and place myself under her protection.

PRAYER TO ST. ELIZABETH

Queen of Hungary

DEAR St. Elizabeth,
You were a Queen,
but you were noble in other ways too.

You were noble in loving your family
and teaching them about Jesus.

You were also noble in helping the poor
out of the riches of your family.

Help me to learn about Jesus
and to be His true follower.

Teach me to be good to my parents
and to my brothers and sisters.

Let me show respect for my teachers
and for all people.

Come to the aid of the poor,
especially the children.

PRAYER TO ST. FRANCIS OF ASSISI

Saint of the World

DEAR St. Francis,
   you became poor for the sake of Jesus
   and showed love for all God's creatures.

You also had a great love for Jesus Crucified,
   which showed itself in your body
   by the imprints of Christ's Sacred Wounds.

Help me to love Jesus
   with all my heart.

Make me kind to all people
   with whom I come into contact.

Remind me to show concern
   for all God's creatures,
   even animals and birds.

Let me do all I can
   to keep the environment clean
   and make the world safe for everybody.

PRAYER TO ST. JOAN OF ARC

Teenage Soldier of God

D EAR St. Joan of Arc,,
at the young age of seventeen
you heard the will of God
in the voices of His Saints
who spoke to your heart.

You always proclaimed:
"Let God be served first,"
and you won many victories
for the cause of God
and the people of France.

You then fell into the hands of enemies
and were cruelly put to death
at the young age of nineteen.

Help me to serve God first
and carry out my earthly tasks
with that idea ever in my mind.

Teach me to love my country
and to pray for our leaders.

PRAYER TO
ST. JUDE THADDEUS

Patron of Desperate Cases

D EAR St. Jude (also known as Thaddeus), you were honored to be a cousin of Jesus as well as one of his followers.

You spread His teachings
and even gave your life for Him.

With good reason many ask you to help
when they are desperately ill
or have some great problem.

Watch over all the children of the world
and keep them close to Jesus.

Comfort all who are troubled
in any way.

Pray that all the members of my family
may remain close to Jesus on earth
and join you in praising Him forever in
heaven.

PRAYER TO
BLESSED KATERI TEKAKWITHA

Lily of the Mohawks

DEAR Blessed Kateri,
   you suffered much from illness
   and you suffered even more
   when you became a follower of Christ.

You were devoted to the Eucharist
   and to the Cross of Jesus
   up to the very end of your short life.

Help me to prepare well
   for receiving Jesus in the Eucharist.

Let me always thank Him
   for giving His life on the Cross
   to gain heaven for me and all people.

Teach me to treat every person—
   regardless of race or religion—
   as a child of God.

PRAYER TO ST. MARIA GORETTI

Model of Purity

DEAR St. Maria Goretti,
 you are a true child of Mary, mother of
 God,
 for you followed her in your purity.

You preferred to die by a stab wound
 rather than to consent to sin
 against the Heavenly Father.

When you were at the point of death,
 you imitated your Divine Master
 and forgave your wicked attacker.

Help me to imitate your love of purity
 and your hatred of sin.

Teach me to be pure
 out of love for God.

Let me always depend on God's grace,
 especially in time of trial.

PRAYER TO ST. PETER CLAVER

Apostle of the Slaves

D EAR St. Peter Claver,
you were filled with compassion
for human beings sold as slaves
and treated like animals.

You cared for their natural ills
and also took away their spiritual ills.

You taught them about Jesus
and led them to become His followers.

Let me imitate your desire
to bring all people to Christ
regardless of their race.

Watch over our missionaries
who continue your work today.

Obtain God's grace for them
and for those to whom they minister.

Come to the aid of all those
who are mistreated today.

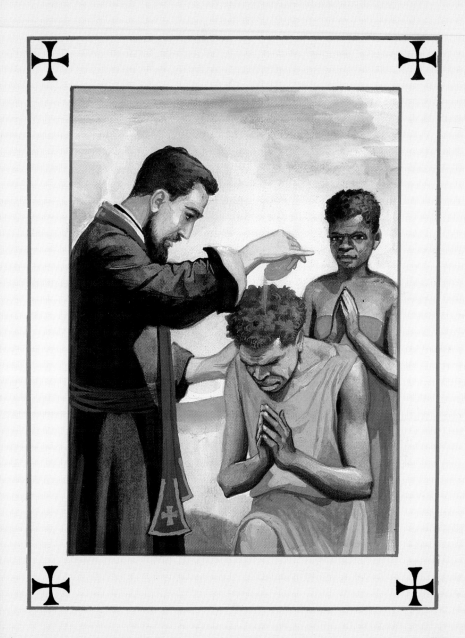

PRAYER TO ST. PATRICK

Missionary for Christ

D EAR St. Patrick,
you brought many people to Christ.

Many of their descendants in turn
spread the Good News to other people.

In my prayer,
I make use of your words:

As I arise today,
may the strength of God pilot me,
the power of God uphold me,
the wisdom of God guide me.

May the eye of God look before me,
the ear of God hear me,
the word of God speak for me.

May the hand of God protect me,
the way of God lie before me,
the shield of God defend me,
the host of God save me.

PRAYER TO ST. RITA

Saint of the Impossible

DEAR Rita,
you were a model wife and widow.

You had many things to suffer
in your life.

Your husband died at an early age,
and so did your two sons.

You were afflicted with a long illness,
and you accepted this crown of sufferings.

You placed your trust in God alone,
and you overcame all your troubles.

Obtain for me the grace
to trust God in all things.

Watch over my family,
and keep us safe in God's care.

Help all the children in the world
who are suffering today.

29

PRAYER TO ST. TARCISIUS

Martyr of the Holy Eucharist

D EAR St. Tarcisius,
   you were a young acolyte
   who brought the Sacrament of Communion
   to the sick.

When unbelievers tried to take the Sacred Host
      from you,
   you protected it
   and were beaten to death.

Obtain for me a great love
      for Jesus in the Blessed Sacrament.

Help me to prepare well to receive Communion
      and to remain united with Jesus in prayer
      after I have received His Body and Blood.

Let me always offer Jesus thanks
      for His great gift of the Holy Eucharist.

Teach me to remember
      that Jesus in Communion
      is the true Food for my soul.